PROGRESSIVE
MAJORITY
ACTION FUND

Voicing Our
VALUES

A message guide
for candidates

BERNIE HORN AND GLORIA TOTTEN

Progressive Majority Action Fund
1825 K Street, NW, Suite 450, Washington, D.C. 20006
Tel: (202) 408-8603

Printed in the United States

Progressive Majority Action Fund books are manufactured by environmentally responsible processes, including the use of acid-free recycled paper.

Library of Congress Cataloging-in-Publication Data

Horn, Bernie, 1956
Voicing Our Values: A message guide for candidates / Bernie Horn and Gloria Totten
p. cm.
ISBN 978-0-615-66943-4 (pbk. : alk.paper)
1. Communications in politics—United States
2. Progressivism (United States politics)
3. Politics, Practical—United States. I. Title
JK2316.H67 · 2012
324.2736—dc22

First Edition

Cover and interior design by GO! Creative, LLC, www.go-creative.net
Copyediting by Jill Klausen, JWK Consulting

Printed on recycled paper using
vegetable-based inks and 100% wind power.

PROGRESSIVE MAJORITY
ACTION FUND

Dear candidates and campaigners,

We offer you this new resource, *Voicing Our Values: A message guide for candidates.* It is part of our longstanding effort to empower progressives who run for office.

Progressive Majority Action Fund is a nonprofit advocacy group that helps turn grassroots activists into progressive champions. We focus at the state and local levels because of their enormous political potential. There are more than 7,200 state legislators across the U.S. and, incredibly, more than 500,000 local elected officials. These state and local lawmakers pass far more laws than the federal government and impact people on the issues that hit closest to home.

Many state and local lawmakers are at the forefront of the progressive movement, proposing the nation's most far-reaching measures. They have made states and localities a testing ground for the newest political debates. And they have won progressive victories with cutting-edge policies—to broaden economic justice, guarantee civil rights, expand access to health care, invest in quality public education, protect the environment and ensure reproductive freedom.

We are proud of the role Progressive Majority has played in making possible some of these victories. Since 2004, our political committee has helped elect many hundreds of progressives to state and local offices. These victories helped flip control of state legislatures, local governments and statewide positions. In 2012, Progressive Majority launched *Run for America,* a campaign that has inspired thousands of progressives to seek office. Our goal is to transform American politics from the grassroots up, to promote equity and justice, and to restore the American Dream.

We wish you the best of luck in your campaigns. Your hard work, sacrifice and courage inspire all of us here at Progressive Majority. We dedicate this book to you.

Sincerely,

Gloria Totten, *President*
Progressive Majority Action Fund

Bernie Horn, *Senior Advisor*
Progressive Majority Action Fund

TABLE OF CONTENTS

INTRODUCTION

HOW TO
USE THIS BOOK

HOW TO
USE THIS BOOK

Right wing groups spend many millions of dollars on message framing. They commission polls, dial groups and focus groups to test words and phrases, and then send their poll–tested advice to candidates, interest groups and activists. The right wing persistently repeats that language, such as: activist judges, class warfare, death panels, death tax, exploring for energy (instead of drilling), government-run health insurance, job creators, job killer, personal injury lawyer, tax relief, union boss and values voter.

And progressives? We tend to use the same language to communicate with voters that we use to talk to each other. That's bad strategy. The most effective language is what appeals to "persuadable" voters. These independent or "swing" voters are the ones who decide contested partisan elections.

Persuadable voters aren't like us. They don't have a strong ideology or pay much attention to policy. They're the citizens least interested in politics. After all, if they understood the stark differences between the parties, they would already have taken a side. Because they pay little attention, persuadable voters are generally unaware of the facts behind public policy. So we cannot persuade them by assuming they know what we know or by using the catchphrases that progressives use when talking to each other. Persuadables simply don't speak our language.

The solution is to frame the issues that are most important to *them* in language that appeals to *them*. The way to know these voters' interests and preferred language is through public opinion research. Good framing requires good polling. It is important to note that using polls does not mean that we moderate our ideology, sell out or sink to the lowest common denominator. Polls don't tell us what to say, they tell us where to begin the conversation with voters. Most of the messaging advice here is based on work by one of the best progressive pollsters in America, Celinda Lake.

Throughout this book, we place suggested language inside boxes to demonstrate what candidates should and shouldn't say. We hope it makes the presentation as easy to use as possible. As long as you understand the reasons behind these words and phrases, we encourage you to adapt them to your own voice. After all, you are promoting yourself—your values, your vision, your commitment. Make the language authentically yours, fully integrated with the knowledge and personal history you offer to voters. Similarly, when given the opportunity, you should add specific examples that personalize the issues; tell a story that helps voters picture the problems you seek to address and the solutions you propose.

Message framing is not a silver bullet. It's just one tool for winning political battles, albeit one that progressives could use a lot more effectively. But if progressives improve the language we use, and do the hard fundraising and fieldwork to deliver our message repeatedly to voters, we will win.

SECTION ONE

HOW TO TALK ABOUT ECONOMIC FAIRNESS

HOW TO TALK ABOUT ECONOMIC FAIRNESS

Every winning campaign needs a compelling "message." This overall message, also called a "theme," is the central guiding principle for your campaign's communications. It's your elevator speech. It answers the question "why are you running?"

Your theme should illustrate the clear contrast between you and your opponent. In various forms, this is the argument that should be repeated to voters through all means of communications, including: campaign literature, speeches, debates, media appearances, fundraising appeals, and even signs and bumper stickers.

It takes hard work to develop a great theme. It depends on the specific nuances of the candidate's background, the opponent's record and voters' top concerns. However, quite a few elections revolve around the economy and jobs. If that's the case in your election, your theme should be something like this:

Say . . .

Our economy is a wreck. To fix it, our policies must benefit all the people, not just the richest one percent. Our system works when everyone gets a fair shot, everyone gives their fair share, and everyone plays by the same rules. My opponent's policies are not fair; they rig the system to benefit the rich over the rest of us. My policies would ensure that every American who works hard and plays by the rules has the opportunity to live the American Dream.

Why . . .

There are more than 40 of these monologues throughout this book. They are structured to express the sentiment "I'm on your side." After all, candidates are not trying to sell their issues, they're trying to sell themselves. When candidates address an issue, they have three ways to demonstrate that they are on the voters' side: by empathizing with the voters' problem, by expressing the same values or goals that voters feel, and by agreeing with the solution voters prefer.

To our detriment, progressives usually focus exclusively on the solution. Remember that persuadable voters know the *least* about public policy, and for them expressions of empathy and agreement on values are often what they really want to hear. Even when voters disagree with a candidate's solution, they may still give credit because the candidate has expressed empathy for the situation and shared values that demonstrate s/he is on their side.

It is also important to start a monologue with empathy, shared values or both because the best way to persuade is to begin from a point of agreement. A point of agreement provides us a place to bridge from voters' preconceptions to our policy solutions. So, all of these monologues begin from a point of agreement.

In the first monologue above, each sentence polls very well. Voters know the economy is in trouble. In fact, they think it's worse than the national economic data suggest. This isn't going to change for the foreseeable future so do not imply that the economy is okay because you're likely to get a very angry response. The sentence "everyone gets a fair shot ..." is a great statement of progressive economic values and it is exceptionally popular. What differentiates us from our conservative opponents is that their policies primarily benefit the richest one percent; ours benefit the rest of us, the 99 percent. Polls show this populist message works. Voters strongly support the American Dream and rewards for those who work hard and play by the rules.

Here's another version of the same theme:

Or say . . .

Our economy is upside down. The majority of America is in recession but the richest one percent is doing better than ever. We need an economy that works for Main Street, not Wall Street. I want to ensure that every hardworking American can earn a decent living, afford high-quality health care, get a great education for their children, and retire with security. My opponent's policies support the rich, mine support the rest of us.

Why . . .

Why do these messages keep referring to "my opponent's policies"? It's not enough to say what you will do; you must also draw a contrast between yourself and your opponent. But keep the focus on his/her policies. Voters don't like personal attacks.

> ". . . most voters believe that "free enterprise has done more to lift people out of poverty, help build a strong middle class, and make our lives better than all of the government's programs put together."

Just as you shouldn't get too personal, don't get too ideological in your criticisms of conservative economics. Yes, it's true that "free market" fundamentalism, deregulation and irresponsible tax cuts have wrecked our economy. But Americans—even a majority of Democrats—favor free markets, lower taxes and smaller government. In fact, most voters believe that "free enterprise has done more to lift people out of poverty, help build a strong middle class, and make our lives better than all of the government's programs put together." So don't attack capitalism, focus on economic unfairness.

More specifically:

Don't say . . .	Say . . .
• Corporate greed • Corporations/businesses are bad • Anything negative about "small business"	• Wall Street speculators • Unfair breaks and bailouts to Wall Street, giant banks, and major corporations • Anything positive about "Main Street"

Why . . .

Voters feel positive toward corporations and businesses—most work for one. Voters believe that businesses create jobs and right now America needs more jobs. Americans especially adore the concept of "Main Street." And as pollster Celinda Lake says, "Americans are in love with 'small business.' It's a concept that voters see as almost synonymous with America." By small business, they mean family-run businesses with five or perhaps 10 employees. The federal Small Business Administration defines a small business as one with fewer than 500 employees, and in certain industries even 1,000 employees or more. That's not what voters have in mind—but don't waste precious campaign time trying to explain the difference.

Don't say . . .	Say . . .
• Occupy Wall Street • Income inequality • Economic disparity	• Richest one percent, the other 99 percent • Economic injustice or unfairness • The disappearing middle class

Why . . .

By all means use the populist language of "the 99 percent" and "the top one percent," but don't identify yourself with Occupy Wall Street. That movement is doing a great job speaking truth to power, but politically it is favored only by the Democratic base. Understand that the "rich" or "wealthy," or the "major banks and corporations" are not unpopular for who they are, but for what they've done. To be effective, you need to connect the bad guy to the bad deed, like unfair tax breaks, moving jobs overseas, accepting bailouts or paying outrageous CEO bonuses. Americans don't begrudge the wealthy their money and they expect some to earn more than others. It's not "income inequality" that voters oppose, it is "economic injustice," "economic unfairness" and people who cheat or rig the system.

Don't say . . .	Say . . .
• Capitalism • Free markets, free enterprise, free trade	• The economic system isn't working for the 99 percent • Level playing field, fair markets, fair trade • Rigging the rules, gaming the system • Stacking the deck • An economy that works for all of us

Why . . .

You don't want to attack the market system because you would marginalize yourself. In addition, there are a lot of economic phrases that, in the minds of most Americans, may mean something different from what you intend. Don't say "capitalism," "socialism" or "fascism" because the far-right has succeeded in confusing voters about their meaning. Don't use the phrases "free markets" or "free enterprise" because they trigger in voters' heads positive thoughts about conservative economics. While these particular words are problematic, the concepts behind them are now central to all partisan campaigns.

The argument for capitalism is that by harnessing individuals' economic drive, all of society is enriched by their hard work and innovation. But that is only true when the money-making operation creates a product or service that benefits society.

> **Today, too many people are getting rich by gaming the system . . .**

vation. But that is only true when the money-making operation creates a product or service that benefits society. Today, too many people are getting rich by gaming the system, by exploiting tax or regulatory loopholes, by dismantling viable companies, and by creating scams that don't violate current law—but should be prohibited. This is essentially how Mitt Romney got rich. This is also how the Wall Street banks crashed the worldwide economy in 2008 and caused the worst downturn since the Great Depression. But pointing out negatives is not enough; voters want to get beyond blame and hear solutions.

So say that . . .

We need an economy that's fair to everyone. That means structuring a system that not only rewards people for hard work and innovation, but also discourages people from gaming the system or passing costs to the community. We need rules of the road that make economic competition fair and open and honest. My opponent wants to tilt the playing field in favor of the rich. I will work to ensure that everyone gets a fair shot, does their fair share, and plays by the same fair rules. If we do that, everyone who works hard and acts responsibly can live the American Dream.

SECTION TWO

HOW TO TALK ABOUT BASIC CAMPAIGN ISSUES

HOW TO TALK ABOUT BASIC CAMPAIGN ISSUES

Budgets, Deficits and Debt

Even though most of the press attention is on the federal budget deficit, which is the responsibility of the U.S. Congress, average voters know that your state and locality also have budget problems. And they want to know what you plan to do about it.

Don't say . . .

- There is enough money

Say . . .

- There are real limits on what our state/city/county can spend
- I support a responsible, balanced budget
- Let's strengthen the state/local economy for the long term

Why . . .

Voters are seriously concerned about budget deficits and government debt. You must acknowledge that you share those concerns and pledge to support a reasonable, balanced budget. However, voters understand that a quick fix does not necessarily exist and that quick fixes often don't prove durable. So you can say that radical cuts are shortsighted and the prudent course is to "strengthen the state/local economy for the long term." Voters do not respond well to the claim that "there is enough money" to fund new programs. Voters believe governments face very real limits on what they can or should spend, and language that seems to imply a desire to write blank checks will undercut your message.

> **Voters are seriously concerned about budget deficits and government debt.**

Say . . .

Our state/city/county has no money to waste. I will pinch every penny I can to help craft a responsible, balanced budget. But I'm not going to cut away our community's future, I'm going to look for solutions that build our state/local economy for the long term. My opponent calls for extreme cuts which over time will inevitably benefit the rich and hurt all the rest of us. I'm for a budget that's fair to everyone.

Civil Justice

The system that handles lawsuits among individuals and corporations should be called the "civil justice system."

Don't say . . .
- Tort reform
- Lawsuit abuse
- Trial lawyer
- Personal injury lawyer

Say . . .
- Civil justice
- Equal justice
- Just and fair compensation
- Hold corporations accountable when they duck responsibility for misconduct

Why . . .

The right wing "tort reform" strategy is to focus on the plaintiff's lawyer and ignore the victim, the injury and the misconduct that caused it. We must do the opposite—focus on victims, injuries and misconduct, not the attorneys. Americans understand that courts must deliver "justice," so use that term. And polls show that voters are actually more worried about the corporate abuse of consumers, employees and shareholders than abuses by lawyers or plaintiffs.

> The right wing "tort reform" strategy is to focus on the plaintiff's lawyer and ignore the victim, the injury and the misconduct that caused it.

Make it clear that what our right wing opponents call tort reform isn't reform at all—it's a cruel shifting of costs from rich companies that caused injuries to the unfortunate individuals who were injured. And that's unfair. Whenever possible, use local examples to make your case and get the focus back where it should be.

Say . . .

Our courts need to be in the business of delivering justice. We cannot deny innocent people just and fair compensation for injuries, especially when they're taking on the most powerful interests. We need a level playing field. My opponent's policies would tilt state law to shift the cost of injuries from a company that's at fault to the innocent victim. I'm going to fight for equal justice for all.

Why . . .

Why say "we cannot deny … just and fair compensation" instead of "we must ensure [they] receive just and fair compensation"? Persuadable voters are more strongly moved by a plea framed as protecting people from being *denied* something than one framed as *giving* or *providing* that same right or benefit.

Don't say . . .	Say . . .
• Give rights or benefits	• Don't deny rights or necessities

This is true in framing a wide variety of progressive policies. You'll see this point several more times throughout this book.

Consumer Protection

The phrase "consumer protection" is itself an excellent frame. Use it to describe measures that ensure safe food, pure drugs, products that aren't defective, and fair dealings with customers. Since voters like "consumer protection," right wingers call it "regulation" and "bureaucracy" instead.

Don't say . . .

- Regulate or regulation
- Bureaucracy
- Washington

Say . . .

- Consumer protection
- Public health and safety
- Make sure the rules are fair
- Enforce the rules
- Create a level playing field
- Act as a referee or watchdog
- Transparency

Why . . .

Persuadable voters don't like the processes of government. To them, the words "regulation" and "bureaucracy" bring to mind scenes of unfairness, inefficiency and frustration. So don't say those words. Also, don't call the federal government "Washington." It's a negative frame akin to "Wall Street."

> **Voters like the results of consumer protection—public health and safety, and fairness for customers.**

Nevertheless, voters like the results of consumer protection—public health and safety, and fairness for customers. So when you can, talk about results. When you have to talk about processes, instead of using the word "regulation," say "fair rules" or "level playing field" or the need for a "public watchdog" or "referee." All these phrases appeal to persuadable voters.

Criminal Justice

When you're talking about crime, you must tell voters how your policies will make them safer, not how they benefit the criminal.

Don't say . . .	Say . . .
• Rights (of criminals)	• Security, safety • Responsibility

Do not begin a discussion of crime with the ideas of fairness or equal opportunity. Persuadable voters want to know how your criminal justice policies *protect* them. Explain how your solutions make citizens safer. That's what all good progressive criminal justice policies accomplish—they prevent crime, reduce recidivism and improve the quality of life for everyone. Conversely, right wing sentencing policies do not make us more secure. They inevitably increase recidivism. And building more prisons to house nonviolent drug offenders takes hundreds of millions of dollars away from strategies that actually fight drug abuse and prevent crime.

> **Building more prisons to house nonviolent drug offenders takes hundreds of millions of dollars away from strategies that actually fight drug abuse and prevent crime.**

For example:

Say . . .

When the issue is crime, I've got one focus: What will make law-abiding people safer? For serious felons, lock 'em up for a long time. But our community is more secure if we focus on keeping nonviolent and young offenders away from imprisoned hardened criminals. Those prisons become schools for crime. Kids and minor offenders come out worse than they were, and that makes our community less safe, less secure. Nonviolent drug offenders, for example, when sentenced to treatment facilities instead of regular prisons, are far less likely to commit future crimes. And that's the whole point of the justice system—to reduce crime. My opponent's policy doesn't make us safer, and the taxpayer costs of prisons are astronomical. It's false security.

Education

Using an array of well-crafted message frames, the right wing has done much damage to our public schools.

Don't say . . .
- Opportunity scholarships
- Run schools like businesses

Say . . .
- Equal opportunity
- The promise of America
- The American Dream
- Educating children

Why . . .

Our progressive goal is to provide a high-quality education to all children so they can achieve their fullest potential in life. The value behind that goal is equal opportunity for all. The right wing program is unequal opportunity and their strategy to achieve it is to set some Americans against others. Public schools are failing, they say, so instead of fixing them let's use vouchers to enable some students to escape them. The right wing also appeals to the market system and urges that schools be run like corporations. But schools are not businesses, teachers are not factory workers, and students are most certainly not products for sale. After more than a decade of right-wing school policy, there is still no evidence that privatizing education—or any of their schemes—actually benefit schoolchildren.

The major difference between progressives and conservatives on education is that we are willing to take responsibility for fixing our public schools while they want to abandon them. For example, say you are arguing against larger class sizes:

Say . . .

The promise of America is that every child will have the opportunity to grow up to live a successful life. That promise is meaningless unless every kid in our community can go to a quality public school. Studies show that smaller class sizes improve student achievement because they allow teachers to spend more one-on-one time with each student. My opponent's education policies would help only a few students and abandon the rest. I guarantee you, I won't give up on the American Dream for any of our kids.

Voters want to hear you stand up for the basic principles of America. Education is the perfect opportunity to trumpet "opportunity."

Environment

In the environmental debate, our progressive values are safety, security and health for ourselves, our children and our grandchildren. The right wing tries to use the value of "opportunity." They mean the opportunity to mine, drill or develop for short term profit.

Don't say . . .	Say . . .
• Opportunity	• Safety, security, health, clean • For our children and grandchildren

Why . . .

On this topic, progressives have a big linguistic advantage: We're for "clean" and they're for "dirty." Common language favors environmentalists because our natural environment brings to mind positive images, the places and things everyone likes: mountains, rivers,

> **Common language favors environmentalists because our natural environment brings to mind positive images . . .**

forests, beaches and wildlife. Right wingers have to outright lie ("Clear Skies Initiative") or lampoon ("tree huggers") in order to gain traction.

In voters' minds, most environmental issues are local, if only because they are thinking of the issue in an electoral context, which is more immediate. That fact allows you to personalize your language—it's about the "air we breathe," the "water we drink;" it's about "health and safety for our children." Here is a generic message that you can adapt to fit the issues in your community:

Say . . .

We've got to protect our community's health and safety, and our quality of life. We understand that includes [keeping our rivers and streams clean. The Big Bend Project would eliminate a great deal of our city's water pollution problem.] My opponent opposes the plan. But I believe this is the time to take the responsibility to preserve the quality of life in [Big Bend]—not just for ourselves, but for our children and grandchildren.

Why . . .

First agree with the universally popular goals of environmental protection. Then explain how your specific solution delivers the security that voters seek. Obviously, some audiences require more facts than others. If you're speaking one-on-one or in a small group, let your listeners ask for more facts. When people do that, they're helping you persuade them. But honestly, progressives almost always give too many facts and do too little framing. Focus more on the frame.

> **Anti-environmentalists want to soften the negatives associated with exploiting the environment, so they call drilling and mining "exploring for energy."**

Anti-environmentalists want to soften the negatives associated with exploiting the environment, so they call drilling and mining "exploring for energy." Obviously, say "drilling, mining and exploiting."

Don't say . . .	Say . . .
• Exploring for energy	• Drilling for oil
• Dependence on foreign oil	• Energy independence

This is generally a federal issue, not a state or local one, but if you're asked about energy prices, begin by empathizing with energy consumers:

Say . . .

Energy prices are squeezing all our families and sabotaging the economy. This is mostly a federal and international issue. But we can make ourselves more secure by investing in energy efficiency and renewable energy which will both lower prices and create jobs.

Why . . .

Don't get into a contentious debate over a problem you can't solve. Express that you feel the voters' pain, mention what we can do, and move on.

Health Care for All

President Obama's Patient Protection and Affordable Care Act is a tremendous step forward. Despite that achievement, the debate goes on.

Don't say . . .
- Universal health coverage
- Single-payer or Medicare for all

Say . . .
- Quality, affordable health care
- Health care for all

Why . . .

> **President Obama's Patient Protection and Affordable Care Act is a tremendous step forward.**

More than 95 percent of the voters are *insured*—the uninsured don't tend to vote. People who are insured are more interested in preserving and improving their own coverage than in covering the uninsured. So use language that includes them in the discussion. Quality, affordable health care is a concept that applies to both the insured and uninsured. A substantial amount of polling shows the phrases "single-payer," "Medicare for all" and "universal health" just don't work with persuadable voters.

If opponents call the new health care law "Obamacare," don't argue, be proud. The law will contain soaring health care costs for families, small businesses and the elderly. Because of this law, women can no

> **If opponents call the new health care law "Obamacare," don't argue, be proud.**

longer be charged discriminatory premiums, more than six million young adults are being covered under their parents' health plans, seniors and people with disabilities on Medicare are paying less for prescription drugs, and there are no more co-payments for preventive care. In short, people who already have health insurance will pay less and get more. And people who don't have insurance will get access to quality, affordable care.

A key provision of the federal law, the individual mandate, will impose a penalty on those who can afford insurance but who don't get it, despite all the proactive incentives. Right wingers want to call this a "tax." But because almost all voters are already covered by private insurance, Medicare or Medicaid, the individual mandate won't affect them. These voters will pay nothing extra. So call the mandate a "freeloader penalty."

Say . . .

Many of us struggle to keep our health insurance, or worry we'll lose it if we change jobs. We worry while health insurance companies rake in profits. The health care law signed by President Obama creates a uniquely American system that contains costs, lets us keep our doctors, protects us from insurance company abuses, and guarantees American families access to quality, affordable health care. My opponent's policies benefit the largest companies and the richest one percent. I will help preserve and protect health care for all the rest of us.

Why . . .

Although progressives know that health care should be a human right, and it's a national shame that 50 million Americans are uninsured, that message does not connect with persuadable voters. Focus on their reality that their own families' health care has become too expensive and too insecure.

Immigrants

When talking about immigrants, never call them "aliens" or "undocumented."

Don't say . . .
- Illegal aliens
- Undocumented
- Amnesty

Say . . .
- Immigrants, immigrant workers
- Immigrants who are not authorized to be here
- Immigrants who are not here legally

Why . . .

Don't say "aliens" because that implies they are different from "us," which is both inaccurate and offensive. "Undocumented" has been thoroughly tested and, unfortunately, it doesn't work. When possible, call people "workers" because it suggests they are deserving of dignity. If you use the term "illegal," try to describe the behavior, not the person. Whenever you're talking about immigrants, also remember the *give* versus *deny* distinction discussed previously. Americans are pretty strongly against *giving* anything to immigrants right now, but you can have some success by arguing that they—and especially their children—should not be denied basic rights and necessities.

> **When possible, call people "workers" because it suggests they are deserving of dignity.**

Say . . .

Our immigration system is broken. This is a huge federal problem that requires comprehensive immigration reform. [The *federal* government should strengthen border enforcement and crack down on employers that knowingly break the law. Immigrants who aren't here legally should be required to register, pass a background check, pay taxes, learn English and go to the back of the line for U.S. citizenship.] My opponent's policies wouldn't *solve* anything. I favor the creation of a federal immigration process that is both fair and realistic.

Why . . .

Polls show that two-thirds of voters support "comprehensive immigration reform" even without a description of it. With the description in brackets above, support jumps over 80 percent. The sentence "Immigrants who aren't here legally. . ." sounds tough, but in fact those are the existing requirements for citizenship. Depending on the circumstances, you might shorten the answer by deleting what's inside the brackets. Keep in mind that three-fourths of voters agree that "deporting all 11 million illegal immigrants currently in the United States is unrealistic."

> **Keep in mind that three-fourths of voters agree that "deporting all 11 million illegal immigrants currently in the United States is unrealistic."**

You might be asked about one particular measure that concerns immigrants—legislation which would allow students who graduate from state high schools to pay in-state tuition at public colleges. The advantage here, and in arguing for other public services for minors, is to turn it into a question of "discrimination" and point out that children should not be punished for the acts of their parents.

Say . . .

I believe our society should reward hard work and responsibility, especially from schoolchildren. If children of unauthorized immigrants have been here for years, stayed out of trouble, and graduated from a local high school, we shouldn't discriminate against them. This is America—we don't punish children for what their parents have done.

LGBT

Let us deal separately with the issues of discrimination against lesbian, gay, bisexual and transgender (LGBT) people and the issue of marriage.

Don't say . . .	Say . . .
• Protect or grant rights	• Fair and equal treatment

Why . . .

The right wing's religion-based arguments for discriminating against LGBT people don't work very well outside of their base. So they try to suggest that LGBT people are seeking "special rights" that are tailored to benefit a narrow group. As with many other issues, it is more persuasive for progressives to say "don't deny" fair treatment

> **The right wing's religion-based arguments for discriminating against LGBT people don't work very well outside of their base.**

than to say that society should "grant" or "protect" rights. For persuadable voters, the best language is "treat people fairly and equally" in employment, housing, adoption, or whatever the issue may be.

For marriage, the argument is similar.

Don't say . . .	Say . . .
• Gay marriage	• Marriage equality • Civil marriage • Marriage for same-sex couples, or just marriage

Why . . .

> **We're simply saying that all Americans deserve equal opportunity, including the opportunity to marry.**

Progressives are not trying to "give" something to gays and lesbians, we're for "equality," which means ending existing discrimination. The phrase "civil marriage" refers to the fact that it does not affect any religion—no church or other faith institution is required to marry same-sex couples or recognize those marriages within the context of their religious beliefs. We're simply saying that all Americans deserve equal opportunity, including the opportunity to marry. For example:

Why . . .

Why is the best message for a candidate "marriage equality" and not "freedom to marry"? It certainly is an issue of freedom and that frame should work when talking to progressive base voters. But again, persuadable voters feel less included in the freedom message; to them it sounds like "giving" freedom. "Don't deny" equal treatment works better with them. Here's a longer answer.

Reproductive Health

When asked, "Do you think abortions should be legal under any circumstances, legal only under certain circumstances, or illegal in all circumstances," about 25 percent of Americans are fully pro-choice and slightly fewer than 20 percent are fully anti-choice. That leaves about 55 percent who are persuadable depending on the "circumstances." According to the Gallup Poll, this has consistently been the case ever since *Roe* v. *Wade*. So, over the years, the popularity of specific measures has depended a great deal on framing.

> **. . . about 25 percent of Americans are fully pro-choice and slightly fewer than 20 percent are fully anti-choice.**

Don't say . . .
- Pro-Life
- Right-to-Life

Say . . .
- Pro-Choice
- Personal and private decision
- Freedom from government interference

Why . . .

Don't say our opponents are "pro-life." They are anti-choice. When we say we're pro-choice, we are referring to the full range of options that should be available to women faced with an unintended pregnancy. This includes the right to have an abortion, which is a constitutional right, a fundamental freedom recognized by the U.S. Supreme Court. There are several ways to express this.

Say . . .

I appreciate that this is a complex issue for the individuals involved. That's why I feel that politicians should stay out of a woman's personal and private decision whether or not to have an abortion.

Why . . .

Polling shows that over three-fourths of voters agree with the second sentence. Research also proves that persuadable voters are more likely to listen to you if you empathize with the complexity of the issue.

You can add . . .

We need to focus on reducing the need for abortion by preventing unintended pregnancies and supporting women who choose adoption.

Why . . .

Polls demonstrate that Americans want to help make abortion less necessary.

All candidates expect to be asked about abortion. But now you also may be asked about birth control.

Don't say . . .	Say . . .
• Churches must provide birth control	• Corporate employers should not deny birth control • Women, not their corporate employers, should make the personal and private decisions about birth control

In 2012, new federal rules re-confirmed that churches would not be required to offer insurance coverage for birth control to church employees. But corporations that run hospitals and universities, including those affiliated with a church, would have to make insurance-covered birth control available so female employees will have the choice whether or not to use it as their method of family planning.

> **All candidates expect to be asked about abortion. But now you also may be asked about birth control.**

A provision of law that allows health professionals to refuse a lawful medicine or procedure to a patient is generally called a "conscience clause." In this case, anti-choice advocates are trying to expand the clause to include the "conscience" of the corporation that runs the hospital or university. Don't refer to "conscience" at all—this is a "refusal clause." Also keep in mind that "birth control" polls a little better than "contraception."

Say . . .

I strongly support freedom of religion. Sometimes churches control corporations that run gigantic hospitals and universities, employing thousands of people of all faiths. Based on federal law, those corporations will not be allowed to discriminate when it comes to individual employees' access to birth control. I agree with that rule because it is female employees of different faiths, not their corporate employers, who should have the freedom to make personal and private decisions about the use of birth control.

Social Services

Even the most basic social services are now under attack.

Don't say . . .
- Give social services
- Welfare

Say . . .
- Don't deny basic protections
- Assistance, support

Why . . .

Again, "don't deny" is stronger than "give." For the same reason, calling them "basics," "protections" or "necessities" is more persuasive than calling them "benefits" or "services." As you know, there is a major stigma attached to the word "welfare." Don't use that word. Even more important than framing the services is framing the recipients.

Don't say . . .
- Beneficiaries
- The poor
- Welfare recipients

Say . . .
- People in need of temporary assistance
- Children, the elderly, and the disabled
- Low-income families

Why . . .

You need to make persuadable voters feel either that they, their families or friends are included among those protected or that the people receiving aid are deserving. President Clinton repeatedly said that people are deserving if they "work hard and play by the rules." That's still a good phrase. When program recipients are called "the poor," voters think of the undeserving poor, the so-called "welfare queens." Conversely, because the programs you support undoubtedly benefit them, freely use the word "families." We are pro-family, the radical right is not.

> **You need to make persuadable voters feel either that they, their families or friends are included among those protected or that the people receiving aid are deserving.**

Don't say . . .
- Seniors
- Safety net

Say . . .
- Elderly
- Basics, necessities

Why . . .

When you're discussing services for older Americans, don't call them "seniors," call them "the elderly." When Celinda Lake led focus groups on the subject, "participants almost exclusively used 'elderly' in the context of vulnerable older people. 'Seniors' now appears to mean a healthy retirement, relaxation, and few concerns." The same focus groups found that people just don't know what the phrase "safety net" means. At best, they think it's about retirement; at worst, they think it is welfare.

> When you're discussing services for older Americans, don't call them "seniors," call them "the elderly."

Don't say . . .
• Free services

Say . . .
• Sliding-scale payments

Why . . .

When a program involves a copayment of some sort, persuadables are much more comfortable when everyone pays something—even if it's a token payment. "The term 'sliding scale' is a cue to voters that a plan is fair and demands responsibility across the board," Celinda Lake explains. "People don't have to pay that much, but it is important that they pay something."

Taxes

Voters are pretty cynical about taxes. They think that taxes are unfair, and we certainly agree that tax laws have been engineered to unfairly benefit the rich and special interests. So don't defend taxes, defend tax fairness.

Don't say . . .
- Tax relief

Say . . .
- Tax fairness
- Tax breaks and tax loopholes
- Private tax subsidies
- Rigged system

Why . . .

Don't say "tax relief" because it frames taxes as an affliction in need of a remedy. The problem is not the existence of taxes, it is that federal, state and local taxes are riddled with breaks and loopholes for the politically powerful. You might also call them "private tax subsidies." Whatever you do, don't defend the unpopular tax system. And don't begin with a raft of statistics either. Begin by empathizing with voters.

> **The problem is not the existence of taxes, it is that federal, state and local taxes are riddled with breaks and loopholes for the politically powerful.**

Say . . .

Our tax system is unfair. The tax burden on working families has increased while rich people and large corporations pocket more and more tax breaks, and that's wrong. My opponent's policies would make the current rigged system even more unfair with greater tax cuts for the rich. My policies are based on the principle of equal opportunity—everyone should pay their fair share.

Why . . .

No one likes to pay taxes and persuadable voters don't want to hear a lecture that taxes are the dues we pay for a civilized society. But people reluctantly accept that they should pay their fair share. Interestingly, a progressive monologue about taxes becomes *less* popular if it begins with unfairness and then goes on to say what government could do

... stick with your plea that the powerful need to pay their "fair share."

with the money. This is because persuadables don't really believe the government needs more money. Talking about the good things government can do with the taxes it collects also evokes voters' biases against "tax-and-spend" politicians. So stick with your plea that the powerful need to pay their "fair share." Now here's an illustration of how to use this language to respond about a specific tax:

Say . . .

You asked about eliminating the inheritance tax. First, let's admit that our tax system is unfair. It is rigged with tax breaks and loopholes that benefit a few, usually the rich, at the expense of all the rest of us. So if we eliminate the inheritance tax, who benefits and who's hurt? For every two hundred people who die, only the estate of the single richest person pays any federal tax at all. Eliminating that estate tax means enriching that one wealthy family, but it also means hurting all of us because our taxes would be raised to make up the difference. My opponent's policy would make the current rigged system even more unfair with yet another tax cut for the rich. My policies are based on the principle of equal opportunity—everyone should pay their fair share.

Tobacco

Despite decades of education, smoking continues to be the number one public health problem in the United States.

Don't say . . .

- Smokers' freedom or rights

Say . . .

- Smoke-free, secondhand smoke
- Health, disease, cancer, clean air
- Protect children, protect nonsmokers

Why . . .

People don't have the freedom or right to hurt others. There are a number of phrases that work for tobacco control, listed above. On the state and local levels, most of the debate revolves around two health policies. First, smoke-free workplaces:

> **People don't have the freedom or right to hurt others.**

Say . . .

We have a responsibility, whenever it's practical, to protect people from harm, especially children. It is clear that secondhand smoke is dangerous and cancerous. Doctors and scientists have concluded that the only way to protect nonsmokers from secondhand smoke is to require smoke-free workplaces. That's what we should do to defend everyone's right to breathe clean air.

Why . . .

Americans overwhelmingly believe that secondhand smoke is dangerous. They are concerned about their own health and it is persuasive to talk about children's health. Less than 20 percent of voters are smokers and even a good percentage of them support smoke-free laws.

> **Americans overwhelmingly believe that secondhand smoke is dangerous.**

The other common tobacco-related political debate is about raising the tobacco tax.

Say . . .

As adults, we have a responsibility to protect children from harm. Sadly, one-third of kids who smoke cigarettes will die prematurely from smoking-related illnesses. The most proven, effective way to protect those children is to raise the cigarette tax. Studies show that when the tax goes up, teen smoking goes down. It's a small price to pay to protect the health of our children.

Why . . .

For voters, de-emphasize tax revenues and focus on health benefits. Legislators are interested in what they can do with the tax dollars but that's not a strong argument to persuadable voters.

Voting

Obviously, we don't have a democracy without the freedom to vote.

Don't say . . .
- Voter fraud
- Illegal voting

Say . . .
- Fundamental freedom
- Most basic right in a democracy

Why . . .

Avoid the phrases "voter fraud" and "illegal voting." Americans believe that voter fraud is a problem even though it's not; try not to reinforce that frame. You want voting to be understood as a basic right like freedom of speech. Just as free speech should never be curbed unless it risks an immediate, serious threat to public safety (shouting fire in a crowded theater), our freedom to vote should never be curbed without an overriding reason—and none exists. Win the frame that voting is a fundamental "freedom" and you'll ultimately win the argument.

> **You want voting to be understood as a basic right like freedom of speech.**

Say . . .

The right to vote is one of our most fundamental freedoms. Without the freedom to vote, we don't have a democracy. Our basic freedoms should never be curtailed except to prevent major, irreparable harm. Because of the stiff penalties we already have in our state, there's really no problem that photo ID could solve. At the same time, millions of elderly citizens don't have a government-issued photo ID and can't easily get one. So my opponent's policies would manipulate election laws with the result that seniors and veterans who are lifelong voters suddenly can't vote, for no valid reason. I promise you I will fight to protect all of our fundamental freedoms.

HOW TO TALK ABOUT THE PARTISANS, POLITICS AND VALUES

HOW TO TALK ABOUT THE PARTISANS, POLITICS AND VALUES

How to Talk About Ourselves

Say "progressive."

Don't say . . .	Say . . .
• Liberal	• Progressive

Why . . .

Polls show that "progressive" is substantially more popular than "liberal." Too many negative stereotypes are connected to "liberal." If we call ourselves progressive, persuadable voters are more likely to listen to what we say. Even right-wing pollster Frank Luntz agrees:

> **Don't call yourself a 'liberal.' Call yourself a 'progressive.'**

Don't call yourself a *'liberal.'* Call yourself a *'progressive.'* It's a smart move. In polling we did following the 2004 election, a generic Republican beat a generic liberal by fifteen points. But a generic progressive beat a generic Republican by two points. Same ideology. Different label. Different result.

In fact, the Pew Research Center found that "progressive" is the most positive political label in America. It's about five percent more popular than "conservative" and 17 percent more popular than "liberal."

How to Talk About the Opposition

When you can help it, don't say "conservative."

Don't say . . .	Say . . .
• Conservative plan	• Right wing
• Conservative solution	• Risky scheme
• Fiscal conservative	• Extreme, outside the mainstream
	• Fiscal responsibility

Why . . .

In America, "conservative" is no insult. The word and the concept are both popular. This is because, while conservative policies are awful, Americans overwhelmingly support stereotyped conservative principles—limited government, lower taxes, free markets, personal responsibility, family values. It is very clever framing. Who wants a bigger government than we need? Who favors unlimited government? Who can oppose freedom, responsibility, or values? When it fits, use the term "right wing." And when you're arguing against a conservative proposal, never call it a *solution*. It will not *solve* a societal problem.

> **. . . when you're arguing against a conservative proposal, never call it a *solution*. It will not *solve* a societal problem.**

How to Talk About Government and Politics

Don't discount voter anger.

Don't say . . .	Say . . .
• Anything that underestimates the level of anger at the political system	• The system isn't working for the 99 percent who aren't rich

Why . . .

There is tremendous frustration with government and politics today. The word "Washington" has become a strong insult. In answering any question, begin by acknowledging and identifying with citizens' frustration and pain.

Don't say . . .	Say . . .
• Government	• Our community, society, America, or we • Common sense solution

Why . . .

While "government" is not popular, "we" are. Another good tactic is to avoid talking about what government *is* and talk instead about what it *does* (or should do). Voters care about ends, not means. Keep the focus on your "common sense solution," another very positive phrase.

How to Talk About Our Progressive Values

Americans believe that values are more than right-wing religious principles. According to an NBC News/Wall Street Journal poll, "values" are about knowing right from wrong, being fair with others, telling the truth, and living up to one's personal philosophy. In other words, it's the progressives, not the right wingers, who stand for American values.

Don't say . . .
- Compassion
- Communalism

Say . . .
- I favor freedom, opportunity and security for all

Why . . .

The phrase "freedom, opportunity and security for all" is a statement of values that polls very well. But more important, it's an accurate and politically potent description of what we stand for. The right wing favors these principles for some—the affluent. Progressives insist on providing freedom, opportunity and security to all Americans. Yes, we have other values like compassion, cooperation, communalism, generosity and mercy, but they don't project strength so they don't work very well with persuadable voters. Instead, those tend to evoke negative stereotypes about progressives—that we're weak and unrealistic. Stick to progressive values that help win elections:

> The phrase "freedom, opportunity and security for all" is a statement of values that polls very well.

Say . . .

Freedom or similar values:	Opportunity or similar values:	Security or similar values:
↓	↓	↓
Liberty	Equal opportunity	Safety; Protection
Privacy	Equality	Quality of life
Basic rights	Justice; equal justice	Employment security
Fundamental rights	Fairness; fair share	Retirement security
Religious freedom	Level playing field	Health security

When you're talking about an issue where government has no proper role—like free speech, privacy, reproductive health, or religion—say *freedom* or use a similar value. When you discuss an issue where government should act as a referee between competing interests—like court proceedings, wages, benefits, subsidies, taxes, or education—say *opportunity* or a similar value. When you argue about an issue where government should act as a protector—like crime, retirement, health care, zoning or the environment—say *security* or a similar value.

In addition, reclaim from the right wing the concept of responsibility.

Don't say . . .

- Individual responsibility
- Personal responsibility
  when talking about a public policy

Say . . .

- Mutual responsibility
- Common responsibility
- I'll take the responsibility

Why . . .

We cannot allow the right wing to linguistically shift responsibility for societal problems from the government to the individual. When they say social problems are a "personal responsibility" they are, quite literally, blaming the victim.

HOW TO ANSWER TWENTY TOUGH QUESTIONS

HOW TO ANSWER
TWENTY TOUGH QUESTIONS

1. Do you favor abortion on demand?

Say . . .

I appreciate that abortion is a complex issue for the individuals involved. That's why I feel that politicians should stay out of a woman's personal and private decision whether or not to have an abortion.

Note . . .

Anyone who asks the question in such a biased manner is not going to be persuaded by your answer. Make it short and move on. For a longer answer and explanation, see page 30.

2. Do you favor gay marriage?

Say . . .

I support equal opportunity for all. If you have two children or grand-children, and one is straight and the other gay, you still love them equally. You know it is wrong for the government to deny one of them the chance of happiness that comes with being married—just because that one is gay.

Note . . .

The equal opportunity frame works best. For a longer answer and explanation, see page 28.

3. Do you favor school vouchers?

Say . . .

We all want what's best for our own children. If parents decide private school is best for their child, I support their right to make that decision. But the parents should pay for it, taxpayers should not. We need to focus our scarce tax dollars on the goal of building top-quality public schools so that everyone has the opportunity to succeed, achieve, and live the American Dream.

Note . . .

Private schools are obviously for the few. Shift the question to the importance of providing opportunity for all.

4. Aren't public employees like teachers, firefighters and police getting too much health and pension benefits that taxpayers just can't afford?

Say . . .

The state/city/county should pay fair wages and benefits—nothing more, nothing less. I do not believe that the teachers, police officers and firefighters in our community are overpaid for the jobs they do. But it is clear that we've got no money to waste and I promise you I will pinch every penny I can. One way to do that is to crack down on sweetheart contracts and outright subsidies paid to companies that do outsourced work for our state/city/county. Let's demand accountability from the contractors, insist on contract terms that are fair, open and honest, and—like public employees—pay those companies at a rate that is fair—nothing more, nothing less.

Note . . .

Polls show that die-hard conservatives think public employees are overpaid but persuadable voters generally don't feel that way. Refer to teachers and other public employees "in our community" because voters are much more supportive of public employees they know, especially schoolteachers, than faceless bureaucrats. Then move the discussion to the related issue of overpaid government contractors. This works best if you can show an example of corporations being overpaid in your jurisdiction—it shouldn't be hard to find one.

5. Do you favor gun control?

Say . . .

I support the Second Amendment. Hunting and shooting are part of our national heritage. But like most Americans, I also support reasonable laws that help keep guns out of the hands of convicted felons, domestic abusers, and the dangerously mentally ill. For example, it's just common sense that we should close the gun show loophole in the current background check system to cover all gun sales, not just sales by gun dealers. [And we should stop selling military-style assault rifles and extra-large capacity ammunition magazines.] We need to do what we can to protect our public safety.

Note . . .

Persuadable voters support the Second Amendment. At the same time, about 85 percent support closing the gun show loophole and requiring background checks for all gun purchases. By all means, appeal to "common sense."

6. Do you favor prayer in schools?

Say . . .

I strongly support freedom of religion. Children can voluntarily pray in schools now and I'm all for that, of course. But government-sanctioned prayer was ruled unconstitutional by the U.S. Supreme Court 60 years ago. It violates our freedom of religion for school boards, public schools or teachers to tell children how or when to pray.

Note . . .

People favor prayer in schools. But they also favor upholding our basic constitutional rights.

7. Do you favor the teaching of intelligent design in public schools?

Say . . .

The founders of our nation strongly supported freedom of religion. After all, many of their families came here to escape governments that imposed religion upon their citizens. So freedom of religion is the very heart of America. Virtually all scientists say that intelligent design is not science, it is religion. That's why children should learn about it in church, not in public school science classes.

Note . . .

Intelligent design is a tough issue because half of Americans believe in some form of creationism, so you've got to lean heavily on their values—religious people value freedom of religion.

8. Do you favor the display of the Ten Commandments in government buildings?

Say . . .

I support the display of the Ten Commandments on private property. But the first four Commandments are obviously religious. That's why our courts have repeatedly ruled, unless it's just secular art, that it violates our First Amendment freedom of religion to display the Ten Commandments on government property. I agree.

Note . . .

Again, lean on our constitutional right to religious freedom.

9. Shouldn't we lock up repeat criminals and throw away the key?

Say . . .

We certainly should lock up repeat violent offenders for a long time. But what about petty criminals or juveniles? Our society is safer if we prevent them from becoming violent career criminals and the way to do that is keep them out of the general prison population. For example, studies show we lower the rate of repeat crimes if we send nonviolent drug offenders to facilities that treat their addictions instead of putting them in prison. Let's focus on what works to make our communities safer.

Note . . .

Focus on public safety, not the criminal. For a longer answer and explanation, see page 20.

10. Do you favor the death penalty?

Say . . .

For cold-blooded murder, I would lock 'em up and throw away the key. I have two concerns about the death penalty. First, there is not an ounce of evidence that it deters crime and makes us any safer, and I want to focus the time and energy of the police, prosecutors and courts on measures that actually reduce crime. Second, there are many people who have been sentenced to death, and at least some who have been executed, who were later proven innocent. That's an awful injustice, and it also pretty well guarantees that the real murderer is never caught and never punished.

Note . . .

As much as possible, focus on public safety instead of injustice.

11. Won't making emergency contraceptives more available increase promiscuity?

Say . . .

I'm for promoting public health. Right now, emergency contraceptives—a form of birth control—are widely available at drug stores without a prescription to any woman over the age of 16. There is absolutely no medical evidence that it increases promiscuity or causes any health problem.

Note . . .

Make sure you understand that "Plan B" emergency contraception is birth control—it does not trigger abortion. It was approved for over-the-counter sale by President George W. Bush. The drug that causes a medication abortion, misoprostol, is a completely different drug.

12. Do you think that "corporations are people"?

Say . . .

Corporations are not people. They are contracts with the state. Corporations are necessary for doing business and our laws should enable people to run businesses successfully. But corporations don't deserve rights that are fundamental to people—like freedom of speech, freedom of religion, and freedom of assembly. Those rights belong to you and me.

Note . . .

It was Mitt Romney who said, "Corporations are people, my friends." The idea that corporations have the right to freedom of speech is central to the *Citizens United* ruling that has resulted in uncontrolled Super PAC spending in elections.

13. Doesn't environmental regulation lead to higher energy prices?

Say . . .

None of us likes it when prices rise. Sometimes new rules increase prices, sometimes they lower prices. But I'd ask your question another way. Do rules that protect the environment provide more benefit than cost? Environmental rules protect something that we all own together—our air, water, forests, and parks—from abuse by just a few people. When they pollute for profit it is at our joint expense. America needs individuals and companies to engage in many economic activities that impact our environment. But we need fair and transparent rules to make sure the environmental costs aren't dumped on all of us.

Note . . .

Make the environment real to listeners.

14. Do you believe in global warming and what would you do about it?

Say . . .

We need to do everything we can to preserve the quality of life for our children and grandchildren. Climate change is real—that's the conclusion of every major organization of climate scientists. It will increase temperature, and also bring more drought, wildfires, floods, and other weather extremes. Climate change requires an international solution, but we can help right here by taking reasonable steps that would cut the pollution that causes it. We've got to accept responsibility for protecting our future.

Note . . .

Progressives say "climate change" rather than "global warming." It polls a little better and it more accurately describes the impact of excessive greenhouse gases.

15. Shouldn't we require drug tests for welfare recipients?

Say . . .

We certainly should discourage people from using illegal drugs, but that plan has serious problems. First, when Florida did this they found that the drug testing costs a lot more than the savings from cutting people off assistance. In our state, we don't have extra funds to waste. Second, also in Florida, implementation was blocked after a few months by the federal courts. Again, we shouldn't waste time and money on useless litigation. Finally, I'm worried where drug testing would go. Florida followed up by imposing drug tests of government employees. What's next? Drug testing for unemployment benefits? To get a business license? To get a driver's license? Everyone in America deserves a measure of privacy, and I think we should respect that.

Note . . .

Polls show that voters support drug testing for public assistance. As of 2012, right wingers have introduced such legislation in 36 states and passed it in five of them. It's a tough issue.

16. Wouldn't it hurt small businesses and cost jobs if we increased the minimum wage?

Say . . .

We absolutely must support our small businesses. At the same time, we need to make sure America really is a land of opportunity. With today's minimum wage, a parent working full-time doesn't even earn enough to lift his or her family out of poverty. Studies show that raising the minimum wage doesn't cost jobs, instead, it puts money in the pockets of people who will spend it, immediately generating business for the local economy. So if we do it right, raising the minimum wage can be a win-win, and I support it.

Note . . .

In fact, 73 percent of voters support raising the minimum wage from $7.25 to $10.

17. Why are you running for office?

Say . . .

The economy is terrible, people are hurting, and our state/city/county is not doing enough to solve the real problems. I'm running because we can do better. Our system works when everyone gets a fair shot, everyone gives their fair share, and everyone plays by the same rules. My opponent's policies are not fair; they rig the system to benefit the rich over the rest of us. I will work to ensure that everyone who works hard and plays by the rules has the opportunity to live the American Dream.

Note . . .

Everyone who runs for office must be ready to answer this question without hesitation. This is a generic example. Personalize it to your campaign and your community and then memorize it and use it every chance you get.

18. Are you a tax-and-spend liberal?

Say . . .

I am a pragmatic and common sense progressive. Understand first, unlike the federal government, our state/locality has to balance its budget every single year. I would maintain a balanced budget. Second, my policy is tax fairness. Our tax system is unfair and I would work to identify and cut tax breaks and loopholes that benefit a few at the expense of all the rest of us. Third, my spending priority is to create a local economy that's built to last. I would work to maintain and improve the quality of life here in [location], not just for ourselves, but for our children and grandchildren.

Note . . .

Don't get defensive. Smack this softball out of the park.

19. Are you trying to knock down the free enterprise system?

> **Say . . .**
>
> No. I will pursue equal *opportunity* for everyone. That requires a system with rules of the road that make economic competition fair and open and honest. I will work to ensure that everybody gets a fair shot, does their fair share, and plays by the same fair rules. My goal is that everyone who works hard and acts responsibly has the opportunity to live the American Dream.

Note . . .

If you're in a crowd you might ask the others, "Does anybody disagree with that?"

20. Are you a Socialist?

> **Say . . .**
>
> I support freedom, opportunity and security for all. We call that a Progressive.

Note . . .

If you're in a crowd, smile. This ideologue just did you a favor.

APPENDIX

DECLARATION OF PROGRESSIVE VALUES

DECLARATION OF PROGRESSIVE VALUES
Illustrated with State and Local Policies

As progressives seek popular support for our policies, it is crucial that we convey the values that underlie our political philosophy. Three pillars support our common vision for the role of government:

First, progressives are resolved to safeguard our individual freedoms. For two centuries, America has been defined by its commitment to freedom. We must fervently guard our constitutional and human rights, and keep government out of our private lives.

Second, progressives strive to guarantee equal opportunity for all. America's historic success has come by providing all citizens, not just the privileged few, with the opportunity for a better life. We must vigorously oppose all forms of discrimination, create a society where hard work is rewarded, and ensure that all Americans have equal access to the American Dream.

Third, progressives are determined to protect our security. To make us truly secure, America must not only stop domestic criminals and foreign invaders, it must also promote our health and welfare. While forcefully continuing to protect lives and property, we must strengthen programs that insure the sick and vulnerable, safeguard the food we eat and products we use, and protect our environment.

Our progressive values differ fundamentally from those of conservatives. While conservatives work to protect freedom, opportunity and security only for a select few, progressives accept the mission and responsibility to extend these protections to all Americans, and to preserve them for future generations.

Our progressive values of freedom, opportunity and security mean that:

1. **Progressives stand for decent wages and benefits for working Americans.** Our economy should provide opportunities for all hard-working individuals and families to enjoy life. Therefore, we support legislation to increase the minimum wage and guarantee paid sick leave.

2. **Progressives stand for affordable, high-quality, health care for all.** The security of comprehensive health insurance should be a right, not a privilege. Therefore, we support the Patient Protection and Affordable Care Act and call for it to be strengthened with a public option.

3. **Progressives stand for a public education system that is the best in the world.** Every child should have an equal opportunity to learn. Therefore, we support legislation to invest in our children's education through smaller class sizes, more after-school initiatives, and better pre-school programs.

4. **Progressives stand for a clean, safe environment.** We must conserve our natural resources both to secure our own health and well-being, and to fulfill our responsibility to future generations. Therefore, we support legislation to lower the level of pollutants in our air and water, and encourage both energy efficiency and the use of renewable energy.

5. **Progressives stand for the elimination of discrimination.** Discrimination against anyone diminishes freedom for everyone. Therefore, we support legislation to eliminate the practice of racial profiling, ban discrimination based on sexual orientation and gender identity, and guarantee marriage equality.

6. **Progressives stand for real security for the most vulnerable Americans.** We must protect the security of our nation's children, elderly, disabled and disadvantaged. Therefore, we support legislation to make healthcare, child care, elder care, companion care and housing programs more accessible, efficient and effective.

7. **Progressives stand for the protection of privacy.** For Americans to be truly free, government must stay out of our private lives. Therefore, we favor legislation to keep abortion safe and legal, and to ensure access to the full range of reproductive health services.

8. **Progressives stand for a criminal justice system that focuses on security instead of retribution.** Tough sentences alone don't make us safer. We also need to deter crime with more police, programs for at-risk youth, education, and rehabilitation. Therefore, we support legislation to strengthen deterrence programs and stop the cycle of addiction by requiring rigorous treatment instead of incarceration for non-violent drug crimes.

9. **Progressives stand for a tax system where everyone pays their fair share.** Instead of following the principle of equal opportunity for all, tax policies often deliver an unfair share of benefits, breaks and loopholes to wealthy special interests. Therefore, we support legislation to eliminate wasteful tax subsidies and tax breaks that are both unfair and not worth the cost.

10. **Progressives stand for an inclusive, open government.** Every American must have an equal opportunity to participate in our democracy. But average Americans are increasingly shut out by the influence of big money in politics. Therefore, we support laws that protect our fundamental right to vote, and measures to reduce the influence of money in the political process.

ENDNOTES

INTRODUCTION

Page 3 "millions of dollars on message framing." E.g., see F. Luntz, *Words That Work: It's Not What You Say, It's What People Hear* (New York: Hyperion, 2007), p. 239.

Page 3 "what appeals to 'persuadable' voters." For much more detail about persuadable voters, their limited knowledge of political facts and their opinions about values and issues, see B. Horn, *Framing the Future: How Progressive Values Can Win Elections and Influence Policy* (San Francisco: Berrett-Koehler, 2008), especially chapter 4 "Targeting the Persuadables," p. 47.

SECTION ONE—Economic Fairness

Page 7 "a compelling 'message'." For a good discussion about creating a message, see J. Blodgett and B. Lofy, *Winning Your Election the Wellstone Way: A Comprehensive Guide for Candidates & Campaign Workers* (Minneapolis: University of Minnesota Press, 2008), chapter 3 "Creating a Message and Delivering It to Your Audience," p. 35.

Page 8 "they think it's worse ..." Quinnipiac University Poll, April 11-17, 2012, Americans believe 68-27% that "the United States economy is in a recession now"; ABC News/Washington Post Poll, April 5-8, 2012, Americans believe 76-21% that "the economy is still in a recession."

Page 8 "everyone gets a fair shot ..." Hart/McInturff, NBC News/Wall Street Journal Study #12336 April 13-17, 2012, question 29, where this statement is favored 71-28%.

Page 8 "Polls show this populist message works ..." NBC News/Wall Street Journal poll, November 3-5, 2011, finds Americans believe 75-12% that "The current economic structure of the country is out of balance and favors a very small proportion of the rich over the rest of the country ..."; ABC News/Washington Post Poll, May 17-20, 2012, finds when asked: "What do you think is the bigger problem in this country: unfairness in the economic system that favors the wealthy, or over-regulation of the free market that interferes with growth and prosperity?" that 56% say unfairness while 34% say over-regulation.

Page 8 "Our economy is upside down ..." Similar to Greenberg Quinlan Rosner Research for Democracy Corps, October 2011, where the statement was favored by 81%.

Page 9 "free enterprise has done more to lift people out of poverty ..." see Hart/McInturff, NBC News/Wall Street Journal Study #12336 April 13-17, 2012, question 29, where this statement is favored by 61%.

Page 9 "By small business, they mean family-run businesses ..." Celinda Lake presentation, February 17, 2012.

Page 10 "By all means use the populist language of 'the 99 percent' ..." Daniel Gotoff, June 20, 2012 presentation at the Take Back the American Dream conference included Lake Research Associates polling that shows 71% of persuadable voters identify with "the 99 percent."

Page 10 "don't identify yourself with Occupy Wall Street." NBC News/Wall Street Journal Poll, April 13-17, 2012, "Do you consider yourself a supporter of the Occupy Wall Street movement?" 16% said "yes," 72% said "no."

Page 11 "voters want to get beyond the blame and hear the positive." Celinda Lake presentation, February 17, 2012.

SECTION TWO—How to talk about basic campaign issues

Page 15 in Budgets, Deficits and Debt "Voters are seriously concerned ..." Matters in this section were discussed in the Celinda Lake presentation, February 17, 2012.

Page 17 in Civil Justice "Make it clear that what our right wing opponents call tort reform isn't reform at all ..." Matters in this section were discussed in Peter D. Hart Research Associates, July 11, 2007 memorandum on civil justice issues.

Page 19 in Consumer Protection "the words 'regulation' and 'bureaucracy' bring to mind scenes of unfairness ..." For this discussion in more detail, see *Framing the Future,* chapter 9 "Talking About Government," p. 113.

Page 20 in Criminal Justice "tell voters how your policies will make them safer ..." For this explanation in more detail, see *Framing the Future*, chapter 11 "Talking About Hot-Button Issues," p. 131.

Page 21 in Education "The overarching progressive principle in education must be equal opportunity ..." For this discussion in more detail, see *Framing the Future,* chapter 11 "Talking About Hot-Button Issues," p. 135.

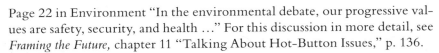

Page 22 in Environment "In the environmental debate, our progressive values are safety, security, and health ..." For this discussion in more detail, see *Framing the Future,* chapter 11 "Talking About Hot-Button Issues," p. 136.

Page 24 in Health Care for All "More than 95 percent of the voters are insured ..." For this discussion in more detail, see *Framing the Future,* chapter 11 "Talking About Hot-Button Issues," p. 132.

Page 26 in Immigrants "Polls show that 2/3rds of voters support 'comprehensive immigration reform' ..." Lake Research Partners, November 10, 2010 memorandum on "Voter Support for Comprehensive Immigration Reform." See also Lake Research Partners, June 1, 2009 memorandum on "Focus Groups on Immigration."

Page 28 in LGBT "Why is the best message marriage equality ..." See e.g., Rutgers-Eagleton Poll, October 6-9, 2011, on same-sex marriage, especially the way language moves independent voters. See also Movement Advancement Project and GLAAD, "An Ally's Guide to Terminology: Talking About LGBT People & Equality."

Page 30 in Reproductive Health "Do you think abortions should be legal under any circumstances ..." Gallup Poll, May 3-6, 2012.

Page 30 in Reproductive Health "Polling shows that over three-fourths of voters agree ..." Celinda Lake presentation at the Take Back America conference, June 19, 2007.

Page 30 in Reproductive Health "Research also proves that persuadable voters are more likely to listen to you if you empathize ..." T. Stout, "Framing Abortion Access for the Abortion Grays: Moving the Middle Toward Wider Support for Abortion Rights in the United States," American University School of Communication, April 2011.

Page 32 in Social Services "Even the most basic social services ..." For this discussion in more detail, see *Framing the Future,* chapter 9 "Talking About Government," p. 117.

Page 34 in Taxes "They think that taxes are unfair ..." CNN/ORC Poll, April 13-15, 2012, finds that 68% believe "The present tax system benefits the rich and is unfair to the ordinary working man or woman."

Page 34 in Taxes "Interestingly, a progressive monologue about taxes becomes less popular if it begins with unfairness and then goes on to say what government could do with the money." Hart Research Associates, June 4-10, 2012.

Page 36 in Tobacco "smoke-free workplaces:" See Campaign for Tobacco-Free Kids, "Voters Across the Country Express Strong Support for Smoke-Free Laws," April 7, 2011.

Page 36 in Tobacco "the tobacco tax." See Campaign for Tobacco-Free Kids, "Voters in All States Support Large Increases to State Tobacco Tax Rates," April 29, 2010.

Page 38 in Voting "voter fraud ..." See generally, Brennan Center for Justice, "Policy Brief on Voter Identification," 2012.

SECTION THREE—How to talk about partisans, politics and values

Page 41 "Polls show that 'progressive' is substantially more popular ..." For this discussion in more detail, see *Framing the Future,* chapter 8 "Talking About Our Philosophy and Ourselves," p. 105.

Page 41 "Don't call yourself a 'liberal' ..." F. Luntz, *Words That Work: It's Not What You Say, It's What People Hear* (New York: Hyperion, 2007) p. 63.

Page 41 "Pew Research Center found that 'progressive' is the most positive political label ..." Pew Research Center for the People and the Press, "Little Change in Public's Response to 'Capitalism,' 'Socialism',", December 28, 2011.

Page 42 "In America, 'conservative' is no insult." For this discussion in more detail, see *Framing the Future,* chapter 8 "Talking About Our Philosophy and Ourselves," p. 110.

Page 43 "There is tremendous frustration with government and politics today." Celinda Lake presentation, February 17, 2012.

Page 44 "Americans believe that values are more than ..." NBC News/Wall Street Journal poll, December 2004, by Hart/McInturff (study #6050).

Page 44 "Freedom, opportunity and security ..." This phrase is discussed throughout *Framing the Future.* Polling about the phrase is reprinted on p. 145-6.

SECTION FOUR—How to answer twenty tough questions

Page 50 "Polls show that die-hard conservatives think public employees are overpaid ..." CBS News/New York Times Poll. Feb. 24-27, 2011.

Page 51 "about 85 percent support closing the gun show loophole and requiring background checks ..." Momentum Analysis & American Viewpoint, January 14, 2011

Page 51 "people favor prayer in schools." Gallup Poll, August 8-11, 2005.

Page 52 "half of Americans believe in some form of creationism ..." Gallup Poll, May 3-6, 2012.

Page 56 "Polls show that voters support drug testing for public assistance ..." Quinnipiac University poll, February 9, 2012.

Page 56 "73 percent of voters support raising the minimum wage from $7.25 to $10." Lake Research Partners nationwide poll, February 2012.

ACKNOWLEDGMENTS

The great majority of message framing advice presented here comes from polls and focus groups conducted by Celinda Lake, who is one of the very best pollsters in the nation.

Many thanks for very useful suggestions from Jill Klausen, Robert Borosage, Crystal Plati, Robert Brandon, Maryland State Senator Jim Rosepepe, Sasha Pollack, Richard Kirsch, Frank Clemente and Nancy Schwalb Horn.

There are several message framing projects that deserve special recognition: the American Values Project; "The True Patriot" and "The Gardens of Democracy" by Eric Liu and Nick Hanauer; the Winning Words Project (winningwordsproject.com); Message Matters (mediamattersaction.org/message); the Hero's Handbook (heroshandbook.org); the Opportunity Agenda (opportunityagenda.org); and the books and articles of Dr. Drew Westen.

And thanks to GO! Creative, LLC (go-creative.net) the creator of the designs for this book.

ABOUT THE AUTHORS

Bernie Horn has worked in politics for more than 25 years as a lawyer, lobbyist, political consultant, policy director, and communications trainer.

Bernie is the author of *Framing the Future: How Progressive Values Can Win Elections and Influence People*, published in 2008 by Berrett-Koehler. He is currently a Senior Advisor for Progressive Majority Action Fund and the Public Leadership Institute, and was previously a Senior Fellow at the Campaign for America's Future, working on domestic policy and message framing. Between 2000 and 2008, Bernie was Senior Director for Policy and Communications at the Center for Policy Alternatives (CPA). Among other things, he wrote CPA's flagship policy books: eight editions of the *Progressive Agenda for the States* and two editions of the *Progressive Platform for the States.* While at CPA, he taught message framing to hundreds of elected officials and candidates.

From 1994 to 2000, Bernie was President of Strategic Campaign Initiatives, Inc., a political consulting firm that helped elect and reelect hundreds of federal, state and local officials. Additionally, he helped win issue campaigns for increased gun control, tobacco taxes and health care, and against casino gambling and restrictions on abortion. Between 1988 and 1994, Bernie directed legislative strategy in all state legislatures for Handgun Control, Inc. (now the Brady Campaign), and served as one of the chief lobbyists for the Brady Bill, drafted and lobbied for the federal ban on semiautomatic assault weapons, and conceived the federal ban on handgun sales to minors. Earlier, he was a campaign manager and issues director for congressional campaigns. Bernie is a graduate of the Johns Hopkins University and the Georgetown University Law Center.

Gloria Totten is the founder and President of Progressive Majority, Progressive Majority Action Fund, and the Public Leadership Institute. For more than 20 years she has directed political nonprofits and led advocacy and electoral campaigns on the federal, state and local levels.

Gloria was recruited to build Progressive Majority in 2001 to help elect progressive candidates at all levels of government. Beginning in 2004, Progressive Majority's mission shifted to focus on the state and local levels, helping to elect hundreds of candidates and building up a progressive "farm team" across the nation. Under Gloria's leadership, the organization has developed into the most comprehensive national progressive candidate recruitment program in the country.

Previously, beginning in 1996, Gloria served as political director of NARAL where she oversaw the organization's electoral and grassroots work and managed its 27 state affiliates. She oversaw the development of the organization's first nationwide pro-choice voter file, and devised all of NARAL's advocacy campaigns, including numerous ballot initiative campaigns, legislative battles, and the Stop Ashcroft! campaign in 2001.

Gloria first worked with NARAL as the executive director of Maryland NARAL from 1993-1996. During her tenure, she was the organization's chief lobbyist and strategist, chairperson for the state pro-choice coalition, director of the political action committee, and was responsible for raising the annual operating and program budgets. Earlier, Gloria worked as the education director for Pro-Choice Resources, as president and lobbyist for the Minnesota Coalition Against Sexual Assault, and as a grassroots organizer on campaigns from the presidential to mayoral levels.

Currently, Gloria serves as chair of the board of directors for the Ballot Initiative Strategy Center and Brave New Films, and a board member for PAC+ and the New American Leaders Project. She is an Advisory Committee Member for the Drum Major Institute Scholars Program, ProgressNow, Wellstone Action and the Women's Information Network. Gloria was named a "Rising Star of Politics" in 2002 by *Campaigns & Elections* magazine and was awarded the "Progressive Champion Award" by Campaign for America's Future and the "Progressive Leadership Award" by Midwest Academy in 2006.